Mellow Mood Mastery

Eliminate Stress From Your Life To Achieve Relaxation And A Mellow Mood

Table of Contents

Introduction

This book contains proven steps and strategies on how to get rid of stress through different types of stress relieving activities.

In this book, you will learn how to reflect on your current lifestyle and find out the causes of your stress. Once you have identified your stressors, you will receive a guide on how to make use of many different types of stress-relieving strategies for your body and mind. You will also find plenty of tips to help you build healthy habits for a happy and stress-free daily routine.

Chapter 1 - What You Need to Know about Stress

The word "stress" has been thrown around quite often, probably by you, too. However, when asked what it means exactly, some might even feel more stressed at the thought of defining the word. This chapter takes care of that for you. After all, it is important to understand what stress is, so you can determine the right ways to overcome it.

What is Stress?

The most accurate explanation of stress is actually still under debate among experts, but to make things easy for everyone, let's consider at its etymology. The word "stress" was coined by an endocrinologist from Austria named Hans Selye. He defines it as "a physiological and emotional response." He derived the term from the Latin word "stringere," which means "to draw tight." It was in the 1930s when Selye encountered the stress response as he conducted studies with animals at McGill University in Montreal.

On the other hand, the widely accepted scientific definition explains stress as "a condition where an environmental demand surpasses the natural regulatory capacity of an organism."

In other words, stress is what you feel in a threatening situation once you determine that you cannot cope with it. The more challenging a situation is, the higher your stress level is. It is important to remember that the individual has a significant amount of control over how the situation affects him or her.

The Signs and Symptoms of Stress

Some people tend to ignore their stress or pay little attention to it because they believe it is a part of everyday life. Unfortunately, experiencing constant stress can take a toll on your physical and psychological health. While it is not a difficult task to tell when you are under stress, the signs and symptoms you need to watch out for should still be studied.

Here are the physical signs of stress:

➢ Fatigue, sluggishness

➢ Rapid and shallow breathing

➢ Heart palpitations

➢ Shakiness, sudden muscle spasms

➢ Muscle aches and tension

➢ Heartburn, diarrhea, constipation, indigestion

➢ Loss of appetite or food binging

➢ Dry mouth and throat

➢ Frequent urination

➢ Clammy hands and feet, excessive sweating

- Rashes, hives

- Insomnia or hypersomnia

- Excessive use of drugs, medication, or alcohol

- Hair pulling or twirling, nail biting, fidgeting

Here is a list of the psychological signs of stress:

- Worry, panic, anxiety

- Anger, irritability, impatience

- Sadness, moodiness

- Racing thoughts

- Difficulties in concentrating, memory lapses, indecisiveness

- Loss of sense of humor

- Excessive absences from work or school, lack of productivity

Why too much stress is bad for your health

Studies show that approximately 80 percent of all physician consultations regarding conditions and complaints are related to stress. In fact, over 100 million people turn to medications just to relieve themselves of stress-related symptoms. Stress also greatly contributes to the five major causes of death, which are cancer, heart disease, lung disease, suicide and accidents.

Sadly, quite a number of people think that stress is treatable by popping pills. Even worse is the ongoing trend of the idea that stress is a sign of success. Some people even use it as a sort of status symbol because stress has become synonymous to being a hard worker.

For instance in 2013, one unfortunate 24 year old woman from Indonesia died after working for 30 hours straight as a copywriter. Shortly before she collapsed, she had been posting online about being hard at work and drinking energy drinks to keep up with work. It is therefore essential for you to understand your body's limitations instead of simply relying on caffeine or medications.

To help you understand the importance of stress management, this section in particular briefly shows the effects that chronic stress has on your body:

Muscular System. Stress causes muscle tension and contraction, which negatively affects the skin, bones, nerves, organs and blood vessels. Chronic stress leads to the development of symptoms such as cramping, bruxism or teeth grinding, muscle spasms and tremors. Headaches, backaches and chest pains are other common symptoms related to the effects of chronic stress on the muscular system.

Circulatory System. Stress causes the blood pressure to rise due to the constricted blood vessels and increased cholesterol level. Chronic stress causes arrhythmia, which increases the rate of blood clotting. Due to these symptoms, vessel walls become damaged and inflammatory cells can enter the vessel walls. These cells release biochemicals that can worsen any existing conditions you may have. Multiple studies prove that heart disease and inflammation are directly linked to stress. Stress can also increase the risk of coronary heart diseases such as stroke and cardiac arrest.

Gastrointestinal System. Stress can also affect your stomach because it triggers the rhythmic contraction of the muscles in the intestines to move faster or slower. This leads to constipation or diarrhea, as well as gas and bloating. Chronic stress can worsen any existing gastrointestinal issues you may have, such as reflux disease, colitis, Crohn's disease, and irritable bowel syndrome. Those under chronic stress often experience sudden weight loss or weight gain because stress can lead to binging or food restriction.

Binging may occur due to your desire to feel better, as food can provide you with temporary satisfaction. The problem with binging is that stress triggers the body to release cortisol, a hormone that triggers fat to accumulate around the abdominal area and boost the size of individual fat cells. Food restriction, on the other hand, may be due to the exacerbation of existing gastrointestinal problems.

Immune System. Studies that show the negative effects of stress on the immune system have been so profound that researchers have created a field of study just for this research called psychoneuroimmunology. The professionals in this field of research delve into the correlations between hormonal levels, emotional states, moods, and alterations in the nervous and the immune systems.

Findings led to the discovery of the relationship between chronic stress and the resistance of the body to viruses and bacteria. It has been made clear that stress causes immune system disorders to worsen, and these include cancer metastasis, herpes, AIDS, rheumatoid arthritis, viral infection and allergies.

Aside from its effects on many important areas of your body, chronic stress can also contribute to the following:

➢ Lowered resistance to colds

➢ Chronic headache

➢ Disturbed sexual performance and interest

Hopefully, knowing these facts did not further increase your stress levels. Instead, you should use this knowledge to inspire you to take respect your limits and take breaks when you need them. The succeeding chapters will guide you in creating balance in your life so you can manage your stress effectively regardless of the lifestyle you have chosen.

Chapter 2 - Identifying your Stress Level and Stressors

Thousands of years ago, human beings had a much more difficult lifestyle. They had to face a lot of challenges to stay alive, whether it was between each other or with beasts. Putting food on the table sometimes required life-threatening feats, such as suddenly facing an equally hungry saber-toothed tiger while in the middle of chasing boars or gathering berries.

In order to survive, the human mind has this instinctive "fight or flight" response; you can either face the tiger bravely or you can run as fast as you can.

This fight or flight response is so automatic that it instantly triggers the hypothalamus – a part of your brain – to stimulate the pituitary gland in your brain to release a biochemical called adrenocorticotropic hormone or ACTH into the bloodstream.

Once ACTH gets to adrenal glands, your glands excrete excess adrenaline, which stimulates your nerves to act almost involuntarily, with actions like twitching and heart palpitations. At the same time, the adrenaline rush enables you to forsake discomfort in favor of the actions you need to survive. You either gain temporary superhuman strength to face the tiger, or you suddenly run inhumanly fast to enable your escape. While neither guarantees success, this handy human feature has its benefits.

Nowadays, your chances of being in a life-threatening situation have greatly reduced, but the survival instincts are still there. It is up to you to manage stress and avoid overusing this fight or flight response. Likewise, if you feel you have been "thriving" on stress, you should know that this needs to stop. Individuals who are fond of cramming before exams or working a few days or even hours before a tight deadline are actually taking advantage of the adrenaline rush, which is why some people refer to themselves as adrenaline junkies.

Measuring your Stress Level

Certainly chronic stress poses a risk to your physical and psychological well-being, but what can you do about it?

The first step is to measure your stress level. In other words, you need to find out how stressed you are. This can be a bit challenging since stress has a multitude of aspects, but it all boils down to the basic formula, which is stimulus and response. Below are the different ways to measure your stress level:

Self-reflection. This entails you to ask yourself the following question: "How stressed am I feeling right now?" While the response may be entirely subjective, the beauty behind this exceedingly simple technique is that it leads you to ask follow-up questions, such as, "What is the source of my stress? Is it anger? Anxiety? Physical discomfort?"

Stress Thermometer. You can also associate a number with the level of stress you are currently feeling with the help of a 10-point scale. Zero would mean feeling completely relaxed. One to two would signify a minimal level of stress. As you rise up until the sixth point, the stress you are feeling is moderate. Around level nine to ten, you are at the brink of extreme stress. Labelling your stress as "four-ish" or "six-ish" can help you guide yourself in choosing the necessary stress management techniques to cope.

Stress Symptom Frequency Scale. This provides you with a more detailed description of your stress level based on the frequency of experiencing stress-related signs and symptoms within the span of 14 days. The scale ranges from zero to three, with zero as "never", one as "sometimes", two as "often", and three as "very often".

The idea is to actively monitor yourself in relation to your stress, and then, at the end of two weeks, rate each symptom using the scale. You can print out the following list or put it on a digital spreadsheet to make it easy to rate each symptom:

- Fatigue

- Nausea

- Increased heart rate

- Excessive sweating

- Rapid breathing

- Tightness in chest

- Shoulder and/or neck pain

- Lower back pain

- Headaches

- Clammy hands and feet

- Skin rash or hives

- Clenched jaw or gritted teeth
- Constipation or diarrhea
- Muscle twitches or tics
- Dry mouth or difficulty in swallowing
- Lethargy
- Overeating
- Colds or flu
- Excessive spending
- Excessive smoking
- Excessive drinking
- Excessive medication or drug use
- Feelings of hopelessness or helplessness
- Feelings of anxiety or nervousness
- Feelings of being upset
- Feelings of overwhelming sadness or depression
- Feelings of hostility or anger
- Increased irritability
- Worrisome thoughts
- Intrusive or racing thoughts
- Sleeping difficulty
- Low libido
- Periods of crying

- Difficulty in concentrating

- Frequent absences from work or school

After rating each item, total your score. This is called your "total stress symptom frequency score." Compare this with the following scale to know how much stress you are feeling. The average score is based on the stress-symptom survey:

0 to 19: lower than average

20 to 39: average

40 to 49: moderately higher than average

50 and above: much higher than average

Keep in mind that some of the symptoms in the list may not be associated with stress alone. If you continue to experience the symptoms and the total score you get is consistently above average, you should consult a medical professional.

Identifying the Stressors

An equally important aspect of stress is its source, meaning where all of the stress is coming from. Change is the general term for what causes stress, but each person reacts to changes in their life quite differently, as well. What might be mildly stressful to you could be extremely stressful to another person.

To help you determine your personal sources of stress, use the following "stressor-identification" scale, wherein you rate each possible stressor with one of the following: N for "no stress," S for "some stress," M for "moderate stress," and G for "great stress."

Here is the list of common stressors:

- Worries or concerns regarding your parents

- Worries or concerns regarding your children

- Pressure from family members or in-laws

- Disagreements or concerns regarding personal relationships or marriage

- Work or career-related concerns

- Difficult or time-consuming commute to work

- Moving to a new residence or location

- Concerns regarding your current neighborhood or residence

- Household obligations

- Financial concerns

- Health concerns or problems

- Death of a loved one

- Home repairs or renovations

- Balancing family and work demands

- Relationships with peers or friends

- Limited time for hobbies

- Concerns with social life

- Boredom

- Concerns with physical appearance

- Concerns or conflicts with habits or personal traits

- Feelings toward aging

- Feelings of loneliness

After completely rating the list, can you tell which stressors affect you the most? At this point, it would be a good idea to start taking the necessary steps to effectively manage your response to these stressors.

Journaling your Stress

Identifying your stress level and stressors provides you with a good grasp of your current state. The next step is to keep a stress journal to monitor your ongoing stress level and recurring stressors. Your stress journal is very important not only for your personal development but also for your doctor, as he or she can use it as a tool to help you cope.

The purpose of journaling your stress is to help you zero in on the specific circumstances that trigger the symptoms. To be more specific, your journal helps you be reflective in your decision-making, organizing, and planning, so you can manage your daily stresses in the most effective way.

When choosing your journal, find one that is small and compact, so you can bring it with you wherever you go. You can even download an app to allow you to create journal in a smart phone, tablet, or laptop.

As for how you write in your journal, it would be best to express yourself in whatever way feels most comfortable. However, if you want some guidance on how to record your stress, here are some suggestions:

➢ Note the date. You can also specify the weather because temperature and light do have their effects on our mood.

➢ Note the stressor along with the time you experienced it. For example, you can write: "8:00 AM: woke up late and had to rush to the office." You can be brief with your descriptions since the sole purpose is for you to take note of what happened.

➢ After writing down your stressor, briefly describe the symptoms you felt, such as annoyed, worried, or angry.

➢ You can also write down the level of importance of each stressor by using a 5-point scale from Unimportant (0), Somewhat Important (1 to 2), Moderately Important (3) to Extremely Important (4 to 5). For instance, you can rate being late for work as a three. Rating each stressors importance can help you figure out whether they are worth stressing over or not, and what you can do about them to minimize stressing over them in the future.

Naturally, the stress journal should not be another stress trigger in your life, which is why you do not have to write in it every time you feel stressed out. You also do not have to write down every single stressor. Instead, set aside five to ten minutes of your time every day to reflect on the most important and recurrent stressors in your day.

Chapter 3 - Body Relaxation Techniques

What is your idea of relaxation? Some might say that taking a beach vacation, watching television, or enjoying a light read are their forms of relaxation. However, another way to minimize stress is to minimize body tension in a methodical manner.

While vacations, television shows and novels are indeed pleasurable, they are more of distractions that provide temporary relief. What you are about to read, on the other hand, are tools you can use whenever you need to de-stress, especially to address physical signs and symptoms.

Body Scan Technique

Do you remember the physical signs and symptoms of stress in chapter one? In this section, you will learn how to prevent and ease bodily tension.

Your body is usually unaware of when it is tense because it has become accustomed to it. The muscles become tense before you know it, and you only become aware of the discomfort once you experience aches and pains, particularly around the head, neck and shoulder areas.

The body scan technique helps you become aware of the tension in your body, and it is very easy to do:

Step 1: Sit or lie down comfortably in a comfortable, quiet place where you will not be disturbed for a few minutes.

Step 2: Close your eyes and mentally scan the body for any signs of tension, starting with the head all the way down to the tips of your toes.

Step 3: Notice whether you are doing any of the following behaviors:

- Furrowing your brow

- Clenching your jaw

- Pursing your lips

- Hunching your shoulders

- Tensing your arms

- Discomfort in your chest area

- Discomfort in your abdominal area

- Tensing your thigh and calf muscles

- Curling your toes

The best part about this simple body scan is that you can do it whenever and wherever you are. For instance, if you are at the office and sitting at your desk, you can do a quick scan right before break-time to check if you are tense.

Breathing Exercises

Proper breathing is a classic recommendation to prevent and relieve stress. Breathing brings oxygen into the body and helps remove carbon dioxide, which is considered a waste product.

The lungs do not actually cause you to breathe. Rather the diaphragm is a muscle below the lungs that expands and contracts to expel and inhale air in and out of the lungs. Every time you inhale, the diaphragm moves downward and creates enough space in the chest to allow the lungs to take in the air. Thus, this causes the stomach to inflate. Each time you exhale, the diaphragm resumes its dome shape. Abdominal breathing, otherwise known as diaphragmatic breathing, is the best way to breathe as it maximizes the intake of oxygen and the release of carbon dioxide.

While the diaphragm is on autopilot under normal circumstances, stress often causes it to change. As you know, the diaphragm is a major muscle. Therefore, stress directly affects it. The result is difficulty in breathing, and the lack of oxygen intake further leads to fatigue, additional tension and higher stress levels.

To check if you breathe properly, you can follow these steps:

Step 1: Lie on your back

Step 2: Place your right hand on top of your stomach and your left hand on top of your chest.

Step 3: Focus on your breathing. Avoid controlling it and just let it run its course as naturally as possible. Check if the breaths come in and out smoothly and regularly.

You will know if you are breathing in the right way when the hand on the stomach rises and falls in a rhythmic manner each time you inhale and exhale. The hand on top of your chest, however, should barely move, but if it does move, it should follow the same cadence as your stomach.

Basic Breathing Exercise. If you notice you have not been breathing well, you can employ the following steps to improve it. Do not aim for perfection though, as this will only cause you to feel frustrated and stressed. The idea is simply to let your body take in enough oxygen and release carbon dioxide effectively.

Here are the steps on basic proper breathing:

Step 1: Sit or lie down in a comfortable position, then place your left hand on your chest and your right hand on your belly.

Step 2: Breathe in through your nose, and as you do so, ensure that the hand resting on your belly rises while the hand on the chest barely moves.

Step 3: Count to three as you inhale in a steady and slow manner.

Step 4: Exhale through slightly parted lips and mentally count to four as you do so. The belly should fall lightly at the same time.

Step 5: Hold for one count before breathing in again. Keep repeating the exercise until you are in a relaxed state.

Deep Breathing Exercise. For more complete and deep breathing, similar to the ones experienced in Zen meditation, take the following steps:

Step 1: Lie down on a bed, yoga mat, or a reclining chair in a comfortable position. The knees should be just a bit apart and the knees relaxed. If you experience pressure in the small of your back, feel free to place a pillow or a rolled up towel there.

Step 2: Place a hand on your stomach and the other on your chest. Release any tension you might be feeling using the body scan technique. Close your eyes to help improve your concentration.

Step 3: Slowly breathe in through the nose, imagining the air filling the lowermost part of the lungs, then rising to the middle section of the chest and finally filling your entire chest. Avoid engaging your shoulders in the exercise.

Notice how the diaphragm is gently pushed down to the abdominal area. Your belly should rise.

Step 4: Exhale gradually through a slightly parted mouth, releasing all of the air from your lungs. Let a soft blowing sound come out of your lips as you exhale. You should feel your belly fall gradually as you do so.

Step 5: Hold for one second before you inhale once more, then repeat the exercise for about ten minutes or until you feel completely relaxed.

Emergency Breathing Exercise. In a stressful situation, you are likely to find it difficult to breathe properly, which is why you should practice this breathing exercise:

Step 1: Take in one very deep abdominal breath through the nose, allowing your cheeks to puff as well as your stomach as the air enters your lungs.

Step 2: Hold it in for six counts.

Step 3: Gradually exhale through a slightly parted mouth. Empty your lungs of all the air and let a whooshing sound come out.

Step 4: Pause after exhaling and hold for one second. Then, breathe as you normally would.

If you still find yourself stressed out after one round of the emergency breathing exercise, repeat the steps two to three more times. This will instantly make you feel better.

Progressive Relaxation

Another form of exercise you can do to help relax your body is Progressive Relaxation, otherwise known as Deep Muscle relaxation. This involves voluntarily tensing the muscles to recognize the sensation of muscle tension. The interesting thing is that when you apply this method, you instantly reduce stress-related muscle tension and at the same time gain relaxation.

Deep Progressive Relaxation. This method starts with tensing one muscle group at a time, and then holding it for ten seconds before relaxing it and moving on to another muscle group. After voluntarily tensing all the muscle groups, you feel immense relaxation. Here are the steps on how to do it:

Step 1: Find a cool, dimly lit, quiet place where you will not be disturbed for a while. Sit or lie down comfortably, then close your eyes.

Step 2: Make a fist with your right hand and begin tensing your right arm and hand. Focus on the tension that starts from the fist and rises up through your arm. Keep it tensed as you bend your arm to flex your bicep. Be careful not to overdo the tensing.

Step 3: Hold the tension for around seven seconds, and then let it go immediately such that your arm and hand become limp. Feel how relaxed your arm has become. Dwell on the feeling for around 20 seconds.

Step 4: Repeat the steps with the same muscle group, then move on to another muscle group.

Follow the same steps for all muscle groups, namely:

- The forehead, by raising the eyebrows as much as possible, then holding this for five seconds before letting go.

- The jaw, by clenching it and biting down on the back teeth. Smile as much as you can and hold for five seconds, then let your mouth go limp.

- The lips, by pursing them and pushing them together as much as you can. Hold the tension for five seconds, and then let the lips open to relax.

- The neck, first by bending your head forward toward your chest and holding the position. After that, move on to tilting your head to the left, and then to the right. The tension should be felt in your neck. Tilt the head back gradually, and then relax. Resume a normal position.

- The shoulders, by scrunching them up as if you are making them touch your ear lobes. Hold the tension for five seconds and then release.

- The back, by arching it carefully. Hold the tension for eight seconds or more, and then relax and resume your normal position.

- The legs and feet, first by raising the right foot until your thigh and buttock become tense. Simultaneously push the heel out and point the toes toward the head. Hold this for a few seconds, and then slowly let go. Repeat with the left leg and foot.

- The buttocks, by tensing them and holding for eight to ten seconds. Slowly release, and dwell in the feelings of relaxation.

- The stomach, by taking a deep breath and holding it. The muscles in the stomach should tense. Then, pretend you are about to be hit in the stomach and tense the muscles. Hold for a few seconds, and then let go.

Once you have completed tensing all of the muscle groups, allow your body to remain in the relaxed state for as long as you like. Let the entire body go limp as if you are melting into the bed, chair or ground.

Quick Progressive Relaxation. If you do not have enough time to do a deep progressive relaxation exercise, you can opt for this quicker version instead. This is a great technique to do during break time:

Step 1: Tense both arms at the same time, with fists clenched and biceps curled. Simultaneously, raise both legs until you feel tension. Around this time, tense the muscles in the buttocks and hold.

Step 2: Close your eyes and scrunch up your face by furrowing your brow, pursing your lips, and clenching your jaws.

Step 3: Pull your shoulders up to your ears and at the same time, tense your stomach muscles.

Hold everything for at least five seconds, and then release. Let everything go limp and allow your body to completely relax. Repeat these steps if you have more time to do so.

Massage Therapy

Are you feeling extremely stressed and wishing for the best way to calm down? Then look no further than your favorite spa. Touch and pressure therapy has proven to be an incredible way to relax the body. Among your choices are the Swedish massage, Shiatsu, Acupressure, Chiropractic, and Reflexology. Find a spa you trust, so you can turn to them every month or so for a one hour stress-relieving session.

If the idea of spending money on a massage stresses you out, then you can turn to these simple massaging techniques you can do yourself. All you need is some massage oil or body lotion. You can also set a spa-like mood by dimming the lights, playing relaxing instrumental music in the background, and lighting a scented candle.

Hand massage. Of all our body parts, the hands tend to do the most work, especially if you do a lot of deskwork. Every now and then, it would be nice to treat your hands to a simple massage to rejuvenate them.

This particular hand massage promotes a relaxing sensation that spreads across the entire hand. Follow these steps:

Step 1: Hold out your right hand in front with the fingers pressed together.

Step 2: Using your left thumb, press onto the fleshy spot in between your right thumb and index finger and move in a circular motion. Keep massaging for 15 seconds.

Step 3: Repeat with the other hand.

Another hand massage you can try helps reduce fatigue caused by stress. Here are the steps:

Step 1: Hold your right hand out, and with your left thumb and index finger, pinch the spot below the first joint of the pinkie.

Step 2: Slowly increase the pressure and make counter clockwise circular motions, holding the pressure. Do this for 20 seconds, then release.

Step 3: Relax for 10 seconds, and then repeat the same step for a maximum of five times.

Foot massage. At the end of a stressful day, your feet might feel extremely exhausted, especially if you have been walking and standing during work. Pamper your soles with an easy do-it-yourself massage for instant relaxation. This is what you can do:

Step 1: Remove your shoes and socks, and then sit in a comfortable position. Prop your right leg over your left knee, so your right foot faces you.

Step 2: Using both hands, hold onto the arches of your right foot, and apply pressure, particularly with your thumbs.

Step 3: Knead all areas of your foot from the heel to the toes. Once you get to the toes, give each of them a squeeze.

Step 4: Repeat with the other foot.

Alternatively, you can use a rolling pin or tennis ball on your soles. In step 2, roll the pin over your soles in a slow manner for about two minutes or more.

Neck and shoulder massage. Your neck and shoulders often experience a lot of strain. Those who work in front of a screen all day tend to get the most tension in these areas. Thankfully, you can do a simple massage to relax this area. This is how to do it:

Step 1: Place your left palm onto your right shoulder, and rub in a gentle circular motion with the index and pointer fingers.

Step 2: Slowly go up to the right side of the neck, and continue to massage the muscles in the same manner.

Step 3: Go back down to the shoulder, and add a bit more pressure to the muscles using the thumb and fingers.

Step 4: Repeat on the other side.

Face massage. The face can feel a lot of tension too because we move our facial muscles many times throughout the day to talk and express our emotions. Here are the steps to relaxing your facial muscles with a simple massage:

Step 1: Clean your hands thoroughly with soap and water. Pat dry and apply face moisturizer to your face.

Step 2: Put both hands on the face, resting the tips of your fingers on your forehead and the heels of your palms under your cheeks.

Step 3: Slowly pull down the skin on the forehead using the tips of your fingers and at the same time pushing up the flesh under the cheeks with your palms. Repeat the massage five to eight times.

Stretching Exercises

If you really want an easy and quick way to reduce stress, then do some stretching! Make it a habit to stretch every hour or so to help relieve your tight and tense muscles.

Easy Upper Body Stretch. To stretch your upper body while you are sitting or standing, follow these steps:

Step 1: Place both hands behind the back of your head and lace your fingers together tightly.

Step 2: Move the elbows close to each other as far as is comfortable for you, as if you will make them touch.

Step 3: Slowly twist the body to the right and hold for a few seconds, then twist slowly to the left. Let your arms fall to your side.

Relaxing Lower Body Stretch. To stretch your lower body, take the following steps:

Step 1: Sit on a chair, then raise both legs as high as is comfortable for you, but with a feeling of tightness.

Step 2: Continue to hold up your legs as you flex and point the toes toward your head. Hold for 10 seconds, and then slowly let your legs go limp.

Alternatively, do it one leg at a time if you find it difficult or uncomfortable to do with both legs at the same time.

Chapter 4 - Mind Relaxation Strategies

When you stop to think about it, the mind never rests. Sure, it slows down a bit during the quiet, dreamless stages of sleep, but it is always working. Stress always starts with the mind, and when the mind is under pressure, it affects the rest of the body.

In the previous chapter, you have learned how to relax the body, so now you can focus on the more interesting ways of relaxing the mind.

How can you tell if your mind is experiencing stress? The tell-tale signs are: feelings of worry, constant irritability, racing thoughts, experiencing out of control thoughts, difficulty in concentrating, and difficulty in falling asleep or going back to sleep upon awakening.

The next question is why you are stuck with these irritating, disturbing, and worrying thoughts.

There are many reasons behind the thoughts causing you stress. These are the most common culprits:

➢ **Eagerness to please.** A lot of people worry so much about being liked, which is why they become bothered when they feel someone is displeased with them. The main reason they are so eager to please is that they measure their value and identity based on how other people perceive them.

➢ **Perfectionism.** When a person spends too much time worrying about failing at something or sets high standards that are unrealistic, that person is bound to experience a life of worries.

> **Putting oneself down.** Those who have low self-worth usually have this measuring stick of what a person should and should not be, and although this form of measurement is unrealistic, they still believe in it. Thus, they incessantly stress over not being "good enough."

> **Fear of uncertainty.** There are individuals who find it difficult to cope with things beyond their control, particularly situations they cannot predict. Conjuring up infinite possibilities is what keeps them awake at night.

> **Pessimism.** When a person has the habit of always thinking that things will turn out badly, they often feel uneasy. They also have the tendency to exaggerate the importance of negative events in their lives.

Negative thoughts are usually automatic, which makes them tricky to ignore. However, you have the power to stop dwelling on your worries, and it all starts with making the choice to stay positive.

Sharpen your Meta Cognitive Skills

When a person has the ability to become aware of his own thoughts, knowledge, and experiences, he or she has good meta cognitive skills. Great meta cognitive skills enable you to control and calm your mind regardless of the stressful situation you are in. In this section, you will go through some basic steps on how to improve your own meta cognitive skills.

Stopping negative thoughts. Oftentimes, you think that once a worrying thought holds onto you,

you can never get rid of it. However, the truth is that you can actually stop it, and the technique to do that is aptly called "thought stopping." Every time you experience repetitive unwanted thoughts, you can undermine them to the point where they are likely to fade away. Here is how it works:

Step 1: Jot down the negative thoughts. Whip out a pen and paper and write down the thoughts that worry you. It can be as real as a traumatic past experience or as unreal as an imagined worry. If there is more than one thought, then list them all.

Step 2: Come up with some happy thoughts to replace each negative one. This can be your life goals, a vacation you are planning, a pleasant memory from the past, or any other creative thought that makes you feel happy. Write down these happy thoughts and memorize them.

Step 3: Stay in a quiet and private place where you will not be disturbed for about half an hour. Sit or lie down comfortably and take a few deep breaths. Relax and close your eyes.

Step 4: Choose the least stressful negative thought and focus on it. Visualize it in your mind, involving all of your senses. Dwell on the negative thought.

Step 5: Shout out "stop!" as loud as possible and simultaneously flash out a large red and white STOP sign with an "X" mark in your mind.

Step 6: Transition your mind into thinking of the positive thoughts you prepared earlier. Dwell on the pleasant thought with all of your senses. For instance, if your positive thought is a memory of a

Christmas dinner with your family, recall the flavors of the dishes you ate. Be as vivid as possible.

Step 7: Repeat Steps 4 through 6 with the rest of your negative thoughts. The better you get at this technique, the easier it will be to stop negative thoughts in the future.

Positive Distractions. Another way to quell negative, stressful thoughts is to dedicate your free time to a hobby that interests you. These can be referred to as "positive distractions" because they let your mind focus on an activity or interest instead of bothersome thoughts. This technique depends on the concept that the human mind can only focus on one thing at a time.

You can do many wonderful activities instead of worrying. To help you out, here are some suggestions:

- Recalling good memories from the past

- Visualizing a plan you have in mind

- Making goals and creating plans toward achieving them

- Exercise, such as swimming, jogging, or working out at the gym

- Reading a book, magazine or graphic novel

- Watch a highly entertaining movie

- Play games or a sport

- Engage in a hobby or project, such as sketching, pottery, baking, origami or any other arts and crafts

- Listen to music

- Do chores at home

- Garden

Be careful not to dwell too much on your distractions no matter how positive they may be. Stick with your positive distraction only for as long as you need to de-stress. Once you feel rejuvenated and ready to take on the world, you can go back to your everyday routine.

Another interesting yet effective way to distract yourself from unwanted thoughts is by using your imagination. This is especially useful when you need to sleep but find yourself too bothered by worrisome thoughts. Daydreaming or using imagination makes you feel more calm and relaxed. If you want to learn how to do it, here are the steps:

Step 1: Sit or lie down comfortably in a cool, dimly lit place.

Step 2: Close your eyes and imagine a memory or scenery you like. Involve all of your senses to make it seem more real. If you have not decided on what to imagine, then here are two very popular suggestions that you can try.

- **The tropical beach.** Imagine a beautiful tropical beachside in sunny weather with a warm breeze. The sky is blue with patches of puffy clouds. There are coconut trees, cool and powdery white sand, and crystal clear water that laps on the shore. You can hear seagulls in the distance. You can smell the salt in the air and the sunscreen on your skin. You hold a glass of your favorite cold beverage in your hand, and you take a sip.

- **The winter cabin.** Imagine yourself inside a warm log cabin with a large fireplace. There is a snowstorm outside, but you and your family are all safe indoors, wearing thick coats and draping woolly blankets over yourselves. You can hear the fire crackling despite the howling of the wind outside. You can smell the scent of hot chocolate and melting marshmallows in the warm mug you are holding between your hands. You take a sip and enjoy the hot and sweet flavor.

Step 3: Immerse yourself in your daydream for as long as you like, and let yourself feel completely at ease.

Meditation Techniques

The concept of meditation used to be about sitting in the lotus position and attempting to float in the air while at the same time muttering words in a foreign language, but the reality is that meditation is simply about focusing the mind.

Studies reveal positive effects of meditation. Even practitioners in Western medicine have come to accept the usefulness of meditation as part of a holistic approach to treatment. This is due to the fact that meditation can reduce feelings of stress and help you control your thoughts. Of course, it takes some practice before you can really notice the effects.

The main reason that a lot of people, especially in a Western society, find it difficult to meditate is their need to stay busy. Being active is more acceptable than being passive, and the idea of sitting and "doing nothing" seems like a waste of time.

Another reason is the need to assess and evaluate oneself. A lot of people are used to rating themselves as well, such as by checking whether you did something "excellently" or "poorly." In meditation, however, there is no such thing. In fact, meditation is the opposite of constantly assessing oneself. What matters is you simply do it.

How to Prepare for Meditation. If you are a beginner to meditation, it is possible that distractions will come easily to you. Therefore, it is important to prepare the right conditions before starting your first meditation session. Here are the steps you can take to do that:

Step 1: Look for a quiet place with minimal distractions, including telephones, computers, televisions, or even other people who are not prepared to meditate.

Step 2: Sit in a position that is comfortable enough for you to remain in for at least 15 minutes. It should allow you to maintain a straight back with relaxed shoulders.

Step 3: To set your mind to a state of meditation, start by focusing on a single word, image, sound, thought or sensation.

Step 4: Continue to concentrate on that single element of your focus with acceptance and passivity. Each thought that is not related to that element should be acknowledged but not pursued. Let that distracting thought drift away like a cloud blown by the wind.

Continue to focus for as long as you wish. There is no pressure or deadline. Once you feel you are ready to meditate, you can move on to one of these two basic calming meditation techniques to help you reduce stress and eliminate anxiety:

Breathing meditation. Do you remember the breathing techniques you learned in the previous chapter? This one is a close cousin to it, except this time you are focusing on clearing your mind instead of the correctness of how you breathe.

Step 1: Sit on the ground or in a chair in a comfortable position, while keeping your back straight and your shoulders relaxed. Take care that your clothing does not restrict you in any way. For instance, if you feel your shoes are too tight, then take them off before proceeding.

Step 2: Close your eyes, and do a quick body scan to release the tension from any tense muscle group.

Step 3: Start breathing in a calm manner. Get into a state of relaxation by taking a few slow and deep breaths through your nose.

Step 4: Concentrate on each breath and start mentally counting each inhale. Count up to ten inhales and then go back to one again. In case you get distracted and lose count, return to one. There is no requirement as to the number of breaths you should take. The counting is merely done to help you maintain your concentration on breathing.

Aim for at least 20 minutes of doing the breathing meditation, and twice daily. You can do this early in the morning and right before you go to bed, or you can do this in between breaks at work. Let it be something you look forward to every day.

Mantra Meditation. A mantra is an utterance, be it a sound or a word that is repeated throughout the meditation session. The word mantra is derived from the Sanskrit word "man" which translates to "think" and "tra" which translates to "free". The mantra will be the sole object of your concentration and by focusing on it your mind becomes more adept at avoiding distractions.

Before engaging in a basic mantra meditation, the first thing you should do is decide upon a mantra. Most mantras usually consist of one or two syllables, where the most commonly known is "om," which translates to "I am." Another common mantra is "soham," which means "I am that." Your mantra should hold a lot of personal meaning to you for it to be effective. Some people even like to use simple, heart-warming words such as "love," "calm," or "peace" as they meditate.

Once you have decided upon a mantra, you can follow these steps during your next meditation session:

Step 1: Sit comfortably on the ground or in a chair. Keep your back straight and your shoulders relaxed.

Step 2: Close your eyes and take slow, deep breaths through your nose to reach a state of relaxation. Do a body scan to release any tension.

Step 3: Concentrate on your breathing. This time, instead of counting to ten, repeat your mantra either silently or in a soft chant during each exhale.

Each time you say your mantra, visualize the word in your mind. Create a rhythm that makes the mantra sound calming and melodic to you. Let your mantra guide you back to concentration whenever you start to get distracted.

Give yourself as much as 20 minutes to do this meditation at least once a day. Not only will this calm you, but it also grants you the positive attitude you can maintain throughout your day.

Chapter 5 - Stress-free Organizational Skills

Stress triggers do not just manifest themselves in mind and body ailments, for they can also come from our surroundings. Many people feel frustrated and stressed out by disordered surroundings. This is especially true for those who tend to spend a lot of time searching for things that are not where they are supposed to be.

Recognizing Disorganization in your Life

How organized (or disorganized) are you right now? Take some time to reflect on the different facets in your life based on the following list:

- **A cluttered home/work environment.** You know you are surrounded by clutter when you keep too much stuff that you do not use on a daily basis. The worst part is that you find it difficult to part with these clothes, books, or even broken knick knacks, even though the clutter stresses you out.

- **Difficulty in managing your time.** Poor time management is when you are often late for appointments, miss deadlines, procrastinate, or always feel like you do not have enough time for everything. A lot of stress comes from not planning your time efficiently.

- **Not having a "system."** Generally, an organized person has a way of handling different aspects of his or her life. For instance, he knows exactly what to do with his finances, and he is working toward building a career or pursuing a passion he likes.

If you find it difficult to manage at least one of these areas in your life, then you will find the following sections very useful. Applying the tips that you are about to learn will pave way for a more stress-free, happy and healthy lifestyle.

Getting Rid of Clutter

To get rid of clutter, you need to adopt a whole new mindset toward your possessions. You need to know what to let go and what to keep, so you are not left with a heaping pile of each. Here are some tips to help with getting rid of clutter:

➤ Schedule a specific time in a week to get rid of clutter. Set a timer and an alarm, so you do not miss out on this "appointment." Create a to-do list help you go through all of your stuff.

➤ Sort your stuff using three bins, one for things you keep, another for things you store, and the last for things you need to donate, recycle, or throw away. The rule is that you should keep the things you use on a daily or weekly basis in your workspace, store the things you need for a specific season and get rid of the things you have not used in six months.

➤ If there are items that are sentimental to you, take a picture of them or scan them for a digital copy if they are documents or pictures. You do not necessarily have to have the items with you for you to recall the memories associated with them. In most cases, all you need is an image of the item.

➤ Invest in durable and attractive-looking organizational tools such as shelves and containers. Create a system that encourages you to maintain a neat and tidy space, such as by color coding everything, labelling your containers, or grouping similarly used items together.

➤ Slowly transition to paperless. Keep books, magazines and files in a sleek gadget to save space. Important hard copy documents should be organized neatly in a safe place, which is secure but easy for you to access.

➤ Learn the one-in, one-out principle. This means you should avoid buying more things unless you can sacrifice one item for each new item.

Manage your Time Effectively

Proper time management lets you take control and feel secure, which helps lower your chances of becoming stressed throughout the day.

To find out how you go about your day on a regular basis, include a daily log in your stress journal that documents what you do in the next three days. Note the activities that occupy your day from the time you wake up to the time you go to bed.

Next, determine the most important parts of your day you would like to spend time on. Also, take note of the parts of your day you are okay without. Here are some common factors that consume your day:

● Time with family and friends

● Pursuing your interests or hobbies

● Advancing your career or work

- Religious or spiritual practices

- Eating

- Exercising

- Sleeping

- Travel time

- Reading

- Volunteering

- Household chores

- Surfing the internet or chatting online

- Watching television

You can also create your own list of common daily activities. After you have made your list, rate their importance and urgency from the highest to the lowest. Finally, determine whether you can delegate certain tasks to someone else or eliminate them from your schedule altogether.

Next, create a daily schedule to determine the amount of time you should spend on each important and urgent activity. Write it down along with the timeframe. Once you have created a routine, test it out for a week and make adjustments where necessary.

If you do not have the habit of making a daily to-do list, now is the best time to start. In general, you can make three types of to-do lists to help you stay on track and avoid forgetfulness that will only cause more stress. The first is the master list, which shows all of the most important tasks and appointments.

The second is a today list, which enumerates the things you need to do for the day. Last is the do-later list, in which you note the tasks you have set to do later on, only after having accomplished the more important and urgent tasks.

Once you get the hang of keeping your space organized and managing your time efficiently, your daily life will be much easier. Tasks will be less exhausting because this time you know exactly what you need to do. You get to spend more time with your family and friends, which makes for a more balanced work and personal life. However, make room for the unpredictable too. The world is a dynamic place, so if some things happen beyond your control, be brave enough to let it go and just breathe.

Chapter 6 - Healthy Habits for Better Stress Management

Our attitude and character is shaped by the little things we do everyday – our habits. In this chapter, you will be introduced to the most effective healthy habits to help you manage stress and enable you to live a balanced life.

Healthy Diet and Regular Exercise

It might seem a little cliché to say that one should follow a healthy diet and find the time to exercise regularly. However, this cannot be stated enough since a lot of individuals still struggle with the habit of living a healthy and active lifestyle.

It is worthy to note that the kind of food we eat has an effect on stress levels. These are sugary and salty foods, as well as alcoholic and caffeinated foods and beverages. If the body is not well-hydrated, irritability and fatigue also set in.

Exercise helps relieve stress because it triggers the release of endorphins, a hormone that helps lift the mood. Notice how after you have gone through a moderate or intense workout session you instantly feel happier and more empowered. Lack of exercise, on the other hand, makes you feel bloated and sluggish.

Sleep for 7 to 8 hours a day.

Inadequate sleep can make any person feel cranky. If you sleep for six hours or less, especially on a regular basis, you will experience feeling lethargic upon waking up, and this will have negative effects on your performance and concentration for the rest of the day.

Then again, sleeping for more than eight hours a day is not good for you either. Research shows that it causes obesity and sluggishness just as much as inadequate sleep does.

The key is to sleep seven to eight hours a day. If you find it difficult to fall asleep, create an environment that is conducive for undisturbed rest. The room should be dark and cool, and the bed should be soft and warm. Noise pollution should be blocked, although you can always play a bit of white noise or soft music if that lulls you to sleep. Avoid becoming dependent on alcohol, sleeping pills, or any other drug or medication to fall asleep because dependency on these will make it even harder for you to fall asleep in the future.

Set priorities.

You do not have to worry about every single thing in your life. Think of your mind as having a daily energy bar not unlike the kind that you see in video games (called HP or Hit Points). This bar will drain each time you worry or work on something, which means you should choose carefully the things to worry over.

To figure out if something is worthy of fretting over, rate its importance and urgency on a scale of one to ten. The ones falling between eight and ten should be the biggest issues, such as having to go to the hospital because of an accident, losing a lot of money, and so on. The five to seven range would include losing your wallet or missing a deadline. The one to four range might include issues of minor importance and urgency such as forgetting your wallet at home.

The rule of thumb is that anything that falls below six should not be something to worry too much over.

Spend time with Loved Ones

Always find the time to be with the people who matter to you and support you. It is essential to have a solid support system full of people who care about you and listen to you. Spend meaningful time with them, no matter how "busy" you might be. You can exercise with them, go on a study date with them, or even have breakfast with them before heading for work. Having loved ones will make even the most stressful situations more bearable.

Live according to a solid set of values

Your value system will determine how you make choices, including the creation of your goals. It is your values that represent who you are now and who you will be in the future. In order to live a calm and collected life, reflect on what is most important to you. From here, you will realize that some things are worth the effort and others should be let go with a smile.

Conclusion

I hope this book was able to help you learn different techniques for reducing stress in any situation.

The next step is to continue to practice implementing these techniques regularly in your life. Give yourself some time to relax and recharge your mind and body, so you are ready to face the day with a fresh mind, a light heart, and a positive attitude.

Thank you and good luck!

www.ingramcontent.com/pod-product-compliance
Lightning Source LLC
Chambersburg PA
CBHW070504290526
45790CB00003B/1084